Christians and Catastrophe

CW01499722

Jonathan Ingleby

*W*ide Margin

Published in 2010 by Wide Margin,

90 Sandyleaze, Gloucester, GL2 0PX, UK

http://www.wide-margin.co.uk/

ISBN 978-0-9565943-0-3

Printed and bound in Great Britain by

Lightning Source, Milton Keynes

Slavoj Žižek, whose excellent book *First as Tragedy then as Farce* has largely been the catalyst for this essay, suggests – with a touch of black humour – that as far as the world is concerned, the 'light at the end of the tunnel' is an express train coming in the opposite direction![1] I am going to assume that he is right and that we are on the verge of a great disaster. Most of the evidence for this I shall have to leave to the scientists, but there are a number of trends which lead, in my opinion, to such a conclusion. I may be wrong, of course. I may have misidentified the trends, or the trends themselves may be cancelled out by other developments. But even if I am wrong, this essay would not be useless, because, disaster or no disaster, we should live as if my assumptions were right! Slavoj Žižek here quotes Jean-Pierre Dupuy:

> This, then is how Dupuy proposes to confront the disaster: we should first perceive it as our fate, as unavoidable, and then, projecting ourselves into it, adopting its standpoint, we should retroactively insert into its past (the past of the future) counterfactual possibilities ('If we had done this and that, the calamity that we are now experiencing would not have

occurred!') upon which we then act today. We have to accept that, at the level of possibilities, our future is doomed, that the catastrophe will take place, that it is our destiny – and then, against the background of this acceptance, mobilise ourselves to perform the act which will change destiny itself and thereby insert a new possibility into the past. Paradoxically, the only way to prevent the disaster is to accept the inevitable.[2]

Prophets of doom, it would seem, have a dual role: to avert as well as to announce catastrophe. Just think of the story of Jonah.

Trends

How should Christian people, in particular, react to this situation? One consideration is that the prospective disaster is a result of a programme which is fundamentally opposed to the kingdom of God. To put it rather crudely, the plans devised by those who are engineering our future are not only mistaken but evil. Even if we feel that we can see a way out – that disaster is not inevitable – the trends themselves are the product of unjust systems which, as Christians, we should oppose.

Here are some of the trends that I see.

• Very obviously, the global threat to the environment is increasingly serious, and especially so for those who are least able to defend themselves from climate change. I am not going to labour this at the moment. It will come up in a number of different ways. One point can be raised now, however. This is evidently a *global* crisis. In the light of the Copenhagen summit and other such events, are we convinced that our *global* institutions are adequate to deal with it?

- Globalisation, in its role as aggressive market capitalism, is producing world-wide tension between rich and poor, as a result of increasing economic inequality. There seem to be no effective institutions to check this. Organisations such as the IMF and the World Trade Organisation are part of the problem. The jury is out on the United Nations. Because it is unreservedly committed to the pursuit of 'growth' and 'progress,' globalisation necessarily puts profits before people.

- The nation state is in decay. This does not sound so bad when we consider some of the effects of nationalism, but we depend on the state, as citizens, to protect us both politically and economically.

- Ironically, 'the triumph of globalisation' creates (often violent) local and factional reactions based on people's need to re-assert identities which they feel are being eroded. What appears to be interconnectedness and interdependency is little more than power exercised at a distance. 'Local' cultures are destroyed or, more commonly, cannibalised to create new wealth (for example, the black man's music becomes the white man's music with the profits going to the white man).

- Those who are essentially critical of globalisation and see it as a symptom of the failure of modernity tend to resort to a postmodern critique which derides the once powerful enlightenment meta-narratives. Postmodern philosophy may be good at analysis but (deliberately) offers no models of its own. No effective alternative to global capitalism is proposed, and as a result it remains, in the public perception, 'the only show in town'. In other words, it is still perceived as bringing highly valued benefits, and these are difficult to resist even when they are gained at the expense of the planet.

Žižek sums this up with brevity and clarity. He believes that, in contrast to the old Marxist idea that people have 'nothing to lose but their chains', the reality is that we are now in danger of losing everything! The trend towards total digital control of people's lives, the reduction of humans to manipulable machines, and, of course, ecological breakdown, means that humans will become, in Žižek's phrase, 'devoid of all substantial content': without symbolic substance (culture), with their genetic base heavily manipulated, and surrounded by an unliveable environment.[3] He has earlier spoken, in a slightly different context, of the creation of 'new forms of apartheid, new Walls and slums'[4] and from a Christian point of view this may be the most serious of all the trends.

A Biblical Perspective

Arguing about the future has been a Christian specialism in the past, something which has brought division inside the camp, and derision from outside. Yet we need to say *something* about the future. Ignoring it ('the ostrich position') seems feeble or perverse. Though over-emphasising disaster might create panic and despair – the last thing one wants in an emergency – denying it, or saying that it does not really matter, when we think we know what terrible things are going to happen, seems worst of all.

Also, does the Bible give us any help here? While the Bible speaks only sparingly about the 'end of the world' – and a great deal of our Biblical exegesis, it seems to me, is wrong precisely because we are confusing the end of space and time in some very final sense with civilisational disaster which means an end in a more limited sense – it is very familiar with the idea of imminent disaster and the need to respond to it in God's way. The Book of Lamentations provides one example. The author, or editor, does not try to spiritualise away the catastrophe which has befallen Jerusalem, and which he (or she) almost certainly witnessed first hand. The fall of Jerusalem and the Exile that followed created a profound theological crisis for Israel, but one which the Biblical authors were determined to deal with. It is because of this that they can help us today. These events called into question something as fundamental as God's abiding commitment to Israel. Look, for example, at the last verse of Lamentations (5:22). Later, Second Isaiah had to reassure the exiles that the Exile did not mean the end of God's dealings with them (see e.g. Isaiah 40:27). Even at the worst times, the prophetic testimony was that existential optimism could rightly undergird civilisational pessimism, and this can be our experience too. What awaits us may be as shattering as the Exile was to the Jewish nation, but it does not mean that God has forgotten us. Nor does it necessarily mean the end of space and time. The ruins of our civilisation may yet be restored – in God's good time.

The Exile is just one Biblical example. Jesus knew very well in his day that his contemporaries were heading for disaster and warned them that this was so. John of Patmos realised that the Roman Empire was heading for destruction ('Babylon is fallen') and expected his people to know what to do about it.

This world and the next

How have Christians in more recent times responded to imminent disaster? The first, and to me largely unacceptable, Christian standpoint has been that we are awaiting an 'end' which will be so radically different from the world we know, and for Christians a so much better world, that the only important questions are how we can escape this world and prepare for the next. It emphasises the *newness* of the new heaven and earth and the new Jerusalem. To use a familiar metaphor, we may be wrecking the good ship Planet Earth, and that has its sadnesses, but in truth the ship is about to sink anyway, and the only question is whether I (and my friends and family of course) have a place in the lifeboat.

There is not much to be said for this approach except that it sometimes encourages Christians in their evangelism. If, it is argued, the only way to escape the wreck is to book a place in the lifeboat and if the ship's demise appears to be imminent, then people must be persuaded that they are in danger and offered a way of escape. I think this approach is far less common than it used to be, and in any case it is not necessarily linked with the idea of civilisational disaster. More common than this evangelistic zeal is withdrawal into the safety zone of the church with its supportive membership and comforting ambience. Much of the discourse among church people is aimed at encouragement and not much at challenge, certainly not challenge to confront such disturbing issues as ecological disaster. This discourse is usually based on the arguments just mentioned. Why should we worry about the ecology? 'This world is not our home' as the song says.

The main difficulty with this approach is the way that it makes *this* life irrelevant. It seems logical to say that if the boat is sinking anyway and life on board has little value, then rescue cannot come soon enough. But that is not how we find life, I suggest, as a matter of day to day experience, except possibly when we are going through times of extreme difficulty. We feel that life is essentially good and has significance not just because of some future good but because of what it offers us now. The idea that the life to come has no significant connection with this life just does not work. If the next life – 'heaven', whatever that means – is where the story really begins, then why not start there? Given that we believe that this finite world and our finite lives are something that God created, are we really prepared to say that they were not such good ideas after all?

In point of fact the New Testament creates multiple links between this world and the next. Obviously, there are the traditional doctrines of heaven and hell, along with such refinements as the intermediate state and purgatory, linked with death, resurrection and judgement of various sorts. There are also strong hints that there may be rewards in heaven, that even those who are 'saved' – again a word used in a number of different ways – may be expected to be rewarded differently according to their behaviour in this life.

What is more pertinent from our point of view – that is, the point of view of those facing imminent disaster – is the way the Apostle Paul links the resurrection life to this life by means of the seed and flower analogy (1 Corinthians 15: 35-8). Clearly this suggests some sort of organic connexion between this life and the next. Romans 8:19-21 has a similar thought. It indicates that the whole creation will be 'redeemed' by means of the redemption of God's people. The text here speaks of 'revelation' (*apokalypsis*) – the revelation of the children of God (verse 19), and the emphasis is not so much on the event as on the content. *What* is being revealed? The children of God as they reach their full potential or development ('glory', verse 21) is the answer. What was always latent in the seed will be seen in the flower. But again, the 'content' of the seed determines the nature of the flower. We cannot by-pass the organic link between them. What we do, what we are in this life, really matters and it matters not only for us but for the whole creation. Startlingly, the creation is not waiting for God to act, but for *us* to get our act together. Paul here reflects a wider Biblical viewpoint. As G.B. Caird puts it in his commentary on Jesus' stilling of the storm and exorcism of the Gerasene demoniac in Luke 8:

> The biblical view of man (sic) is that God intended him to be lord of nature (Genesis 1:26, Psalm 8) and because he has by sin forfeited his viceregal throne, nature displays signs of disorder parallel to those in human life...From this intimate association of man and nature in their relationship to the mystery of iniquity it followed that the redemption of man would be accompanied by the restoration of paradise: the wolf would dwell with the lamb and the desert would blossom as a rose (Isaiah 11:6-9, 35, 55:12-18).[5]

Experience and Memory

I am here greatly attracted to C. S. Lewis's suggestion that this has something to do with 'experience' or the memory of our experience.[6] What we take with us – the DNA of the seed that is planted when we die, so to speak – is a memory, a perfect memory, it may be, of our actual experiences. This is the raw material from which our lives will be reconstructed in the new heaven and earth. Some of the memories will be good – acts of courage and compassion, for example – and some will be bad: 'diamonds and rust' as Joan Baez put it, in a famous song of that name. The bad memories will need to be healed through forgiveness and integration. The end of the process will be the creation of a new world. Memory drags with it those remembered, who are also 'resurrected'. The key remains experience. What I am trying to emphasise here is the way that this life 'constitutes' the next. That is why relationship matters. That is why care for the creation is important. That is why people should not be allowed to live in slums, for example. Our 'idea' of this life becomes our 'idea' of the next.

In his letter to the Philippians, Paul, himself in prison and in danger of execution, is clearly thinking hard about matters of life and death. He wants to 'attain the resurrection' he says, and he will do this by sharing in Christ's sufferings (3:10,11). If he stands in solidity with Christ through imprisonment and persecution, then he has those experiences to take with him, it is a 'resurrection' for him, when the time comes. He also speaks about the believers at Philippi as his 'crown' (4:1), meaning a party hat, not a crown denoting authority. When the good times come, it is the Philippians and people like them, who will make the party worth going to. In this way we may carry our own future with us. Paul says this when he speaks about the judgement of believers by Christ (2 Corinthians 5:10). At that tribunal we shall 'receive what is ours' or 'receive what we own ' (*komizetai*) . Some of what we have done will be precious and some of it will be rubbish (1 Corinthians

3:12-15). Diamonds and rust again! Out of the materials we bring with us we build the future.

Rescuing the creation

It is in this sense that I think we can speak more positively about a 'lifeboat theology'. Suppose we are in a situation in which the disaster has already struck. Then what? Let me share some thoughts here inspired by Mike Scott's 'The Wind in the Wires'. The song envisages two people who are escaping from a catastrophe. It links, in Scott's mind, with 'the day of the Lord' in the Bible – the song's refrain is 'This is the day' – but like the event that the prophet Amos describes (Amos 5:18) it is 'a day of darkness and not light'. So 'the day', in Scott's song, is a dark and stormy one. There is, however, just one glimmer of hope.

> Swim, lady, swim,
> lady, don't refuse,
> though our chances are slim
> and we're totally confused
> there are clues to be found
> and I'd ask my peers
> but they're all dumbing down
> 'till this bad weather clears.[7]

The flood is upon them but nobody wants to know. Like today, people are just keeping their heads down and hoping that the trouble will pass. What hope there is in the situation lies, it seems to me, within the two would-be escapees.

It is not simply a matter as to whether they will escape the danger; the fate of the whole civilisation which they represent depends on them. If they do not escape, not only will they perish, but so will everybody else. I admit that this all sounds like a crazy fantasy, the dream of megalomaniacs, and of course it may be. The fate of the world may have nothing to do with us. (Though the Apostle Paul would not agree, see again Romans 8:19-23). The very fact that it is a dream which can be dreamt, however, means that it has something to offer. As the song says:

> and if it's all in our minds
> well – where else would it be?

I am offering only an imagined raft, you might say. But what else is on offer? Apart from the raft there is only the sea.

Thus we Christians are, it seems to me, both the escapees from, and the saviours of, our civilisation. It is we who have to escape, but it is also we who must remain, because we have the memories of what is worth remembering about that now-disintegrating world. And in one very important sense, that is the only world we have got, which is why we have to hold onto it.

Of course, our world *is* being destroyed – nobody doubts that. We just have to look around us. Already we see catastrophe piled on catastrophe. Perhaps it is true, as I have suggested, that the only hope for the survival of this world is the memories we carry with us. This paradox is beautifully described in C. S. Lewis's *The Last Battle.*[8] Narnia is being systematically destroyed. Jill and Eustace and their companions are called upon to fight to the last to try and save it. But they fail. Night falls on Narnia. Nevertheless it is in them that Narnia is resurrected. In the same way, our world, though it is being destroyed, is the only world that we have got. We must fight to save it in the hope that we shall see it again.

Living in the here and now

What all this means, rather surprisingly, is that the New Testament has very little to say about the next life. What matters is the here and now. There may be death and disaster just round the corner but that is all the more reason for getting busy. Jesus knew that his death was imminent, and that it was likely that his offer of the kingdom would not be accepted, but the offer was made all the same. Judas was caught up in purposes that were bigger than his understanding, but his betrayal still mattered. James speaks in his letter of 'the coming of the Lord' but only after he has attacked the rich for their exploitation of their workers and their luxurious lifestyle (James 5:1-7). Peter announces suddenly that 'the end of all things is near' but he certainly does not consider this a reason to down tools. It is all the more necessary, he says, to be serious and disciplined (1 Peter 4:7).

So here is a second possible response to 'the end'. In terms of our analogy we must do whatever we can to keep the ship afloat, however much it might appear that it is about to sink. Life is a miracle, experience is valuable, the world we live in is unique and uniquely precious. Life, experience, the created world itself are not disposables to be sent to landfill, though they may have to be recycled. The quality of our relationships is also highly significant. What Paul calls 'the works of the flesh' – such matters as enmities, strife, jealousy, anger, quarrels, dissensions, factions, envy – cannot inherit the kingdom of God (Galatians 5:19-21). They, if anything, are what go to the eternal rubbish dump. Paul, however, sticks to his agricultural metaphor. He puts everything under the simple rubric 'you reap whatever you sow' (Galatians 6:7). So we are back to the seed and flower illustration again.

In sum, however much we are convinced that ecological disaster is inevitable, it is still our responsibility to try to prolong the world's life and to save the environment. Apart from anything else it is the only environment we have in which to learn to be fully human. Survival, in this sense, is a hugely important goal – especially for Christians. I would make one exception, however, to that general rule, and it is a crucial one. Because relationships are at the heart of all this, we can say that even more important than survival is justice. However much we must struggle to keep things going we must not do so at the cost of behaving unjustly. Walter Wink has pointed out that whenever a 'power' becomes committed to its own survival as 'the bottom line', it becomes demonic.[9] We can see this on an international scale when a nation like Israel abandons justice for its neighbours in the name of security. Indeed, why pick on Israel? Much larger and less threatened nations have recently swapped justice for security and continue to do so. On an individual level, it is a Christian principle, one which Jesus demonstrated supremely, that 'one lays down one's life for one's friends', the opposite of a policy of survival at all costs. Besides, justice and sacrifice are often linked. The environmental crisis which is upon us will be felt first and most profoundly by the poorer nations in the Global South. It is a matter of justice that their survival be the first consideration, and that the West, who are largely responsible for the crisis, be prepared to sacrifice in order to ensure it. 'The polluter pays' is a just principle, and one which we cannot simply skip over because we are too busy securing our own safety.

The techno fix

When I say that we must do everything possible to save the planet I do not mean to imply that I think that if we are ingenious enough we can find some technology which will defuse the crisis altogether. This may be so – nothing is impossible – but I think it unlikely. In fact I suspect that this kind of thinking is often similar to the wrong sort of 'new heaven and earth' approach, by which we calculate that we can look forward to a new world, built by our new technologies, so that it does not matter very much what we do to this one. At its most extreme we have what I call the 'science fiction' solution, which might even include abandoning this planet for another one! While we may think this is ridiculous, it is not very far from the approach of the WWF or a progressive journalist like George Monbiot who survey the various causes of our ecological distress and then suggest that it we put enough of them right (by means of technological innovation, it may be) then we can create 'a new world' safe for us to live in. Of course, it does seem right that scientific ingenuity, which has been put at the disposal to such a large extent of humans bent on destruction, should be harnessed to contribute to human survival. ('You got us into this mess, now you get us out of it'.)

I have several reasons for doubting whether this way of thinking is a sensible one, however. First of all, the idea that there is a 'magic bullet' (or a number of them) coming soon is not a responsible way to look at the future. It creates a false optimism which can replace a sober attempt to evaluate the situation and respond accordingly. In Doris Lessing's *The Making of the Representative for Planet 8*,[10] the inhabitants of the planet know that a catastrophe is coming – a new ice age – but also feel assured that the agent who has been sent to them by Canopus, the superior civilisation, is preparing them for a great escape, probably the arrival of a space ship which will take them all to safety. Despite the agent's repeated warning that there is no such plan, they go on believing in it. It is only when the agent himself dies (as do, in due course, all the rest of the population) that it becomes clear that there will be no rescue.

What adds to the power of the fable is that even the lesser technology – a wall that they build themselves under the agent's instructions and which they believe is an impregnable barrier against the ice – cannot save them. We, in our civilisation may smile at the Science Fiction solutions that people come up with – our equivalent of a space ship from another planet – but nevertheless have great faith in our own more mundane technology, without any real evidence that it can make the crucial difference.

What makes me even more suspicious of the 'technical fix' is that we too often promote it as the driving force of effective change, when it is actually no more than one possible means of that change and not its cause. As Walter Benjamin so clearly saw (and so brilliantly described) the 'angel of history' is not propelled forward into the future by rational considerations, or if it is, it is powerless to follow these promptings. It might want to go back and mend the wreckage that our civilisation is creating but it is blown onwards into the future by the wind of Progress.[11] This is a poetic way of saying that we are captive to ideologies which are much more pervasive and powerful than any carefully laid out plan based on the latest technology. We simply never get to the place where these plans can be implemented. As the writer of the old hymn says: 'Other lords have long held sway', or as the Apostle Paul said 'you were carried away by dumb idols' (1 Corinthians 12:2). In our day these are the idols of greed ('don't mess with my standard of living') and fear ('don't threaten my security') and pride ('of course we can fix it') and they gain their strength from lies such as the inevitability of progress and that prosperity can be gained at the expense of my neighbour, without there being any consequences.

No. Technology will not save us. This is the train we are on and we cannot stop at the station for repairs or exchange it for another. It is a runaway train. There came a moment, not so long ago, when we discarded the brakes and opted for a train that year by year, decade by decade, would travel faster (we call this 'growth'). Now that we are travelling too fast, or that we are likely to crash, we find that there are no brakes, or if there are we do not have the will to use them.

In fact there is an answer, a reasonable account of what we might do, though the voice that commends it is very faint. It prescribes socialism rather than capitalism, distribution instead of growth, local solutions rather than global ones, limits rather than excess, regulation instead of deregulation, cooperation instead of competition, instruments of production instead of weapons of war and so on. But who really believes in all that stuff nowadays? Even my Christian friends are happy to defend capitalism, 'growth', conspicuous consumption (think about Christmas!), a world without rules, competition, the arms industry ('we must have the right to defend ourselves') – and that is only a brief list of our follies.

Allies

Is there any hope for our world? Possibly not, but in resisting the destruction we see all around us, as we have repeatedly said, this is no time to quit. We need to muster all the available forces, and it is striking that there is everywhere a stirring of protest by people from a wide variety of standpoints and backgrounds. Žižek quite remarkably proposes an alliance between Christians and radicals.

> Although Christian fundamentalist apocalyptism is considered the most ridiculous and dangerous [of the various versions of apocalyptism], it remains the version closest to radical 'millenarian' emancipatory logic. The task is thus to bring it into closer contact with secular ecologism, thereby conceiving the threat of annihilation as the chance for a radical emancipatory renewal.[12]

It would have been helpful if Žižek had written in more detail about the 'radical emancipatory renewal' he has in mind, but, failing that, it seems good to take his ideas a little further.

Žižek's two hoped-for allies are 'Christian fundamentalist apocalyptism' (we can omit the term 'fundamentalist' henceforth without changing the direction of Žižek's argument) and 'secular ecologism'. By the latter we can assume that he means those who, without benefit of theology, are trying to tend the planet, in much the same way that a keen gardener lovingly cares for a well established garden, or a prudent householder looks after a property that is a necessary bulwark against ending up on the street. People, in fact, who are defending their homes, both because they are places they need to live in and because they are a source of pleasure and meaning. Christian apocalypsists, on the other hand, more likely link the defence of the planet with a vision of some future good and the possibility of renewal. Paul's wonderful phrase 'renewed in the image of the Creator' (Colossians 3:10) comes to mind. Though this text is not specifically about the renewal of the creation; it is about the renewal of Christian character (see verses 5-10 for a fuller context). In the light of our contention that right relationships are central to the resurrection 'project' ('you reap what you sow') the statement still has its relevance. I have already tried to show how this might work, but whether the mechanism is rightly described is not really the main point here. What is of paramount importance is that neither secular ecologists nor Christian apocalypsists feel that they can give up on the world. They are therefore *allies* against the forces of destruction. Not only can they not give up, but they *do not have to give up*. They can get beyond a grim last-stand resistance, admirable as that might be, and offer a hope 'by which we are saved' (Romans 8:24).

As I say, we should recognise that this hope is not just typical of Christians. Many secular ecologists believe that the earth will outlast the assaults of the human race after human civilisation has crashed. In the eco-thriller *Edge of Darkness* the heroine, an environmental scientist and radical activist, assures her bewildered policeman father that despite what humans are doing, the planet will protect itself. According to her, millions of years before humans were even heard of, the planet faced a destructive crisis similar to today's, only on this occasion it was an all-encompassing ice age. It was saved by the spread of black flowers that rapidly covered the surface of the earth, sucking in the heat and energy of the sun. *Edge of Darkness* is a powerful fable, not only because it takes the possibility of a nuclear conflagration seriously, but because it pits the GAIA organisation – environmentalists working to save the planet – against the nuclear-military-industrial establishment. At the same time that we hear about the planet saving itself, we are listening to a speech by a nuclear entrepreneur who sees no future for the earth. Instead he hopes to harness nuclear fusion to provide the power for spaceships that will enable the human race to escape from 'this overpopulated, over exhausted plant'. In order to achieve this nuclear empire, all means are permissible, including the ruthless removal of any sort of opposition. Not surprisingly, in response the GAIA organisation develops a revolutionary edge – and so we have a first rate thriller on our hands.

Žižek mentions as part of his suggestion that secular ecologists and Christian apocalypsists should make common cause, that the purpose of this would be a new 'radical emancipatory politics'. This is exactly right. It is not just that we have the same goals but also that together we must fight the system. The Empire needs not only to be recognised, but to be resisted, and in doing this we need all the help we can get from likeminded people. At the very least Christians should be joining, and playing a full part in, the various 'green' initiatives that are springing up today. Yet there is more to it than that. We are living in a fallen world. The 'world', in the way that the New Testament often uses the term, is a Domination System, as Walter Wink points out[13] which is powerful, destructive and also ephemeral.

The first Christians and Matthew 24

The very first Christians knew about this. No sooner had they begun to follow The Way than they were thrown into a situation of great crisis. Despite the growth of the church in the rest of the Roman Empire, Christians in the homeland, Palestine, were soon trapped in a nation that was heading for disaster. As far as we can tell they were prepared for this by the teaching of Jesus himself. Matthew chapter 24 (and parallels) is one example of such teaching. This has immense value for us as Christians today as we too join the battle in a crisis situation.

The crisis described in Matthew 24 has the usual mixture of opportunity and danger, it is also a time of judgement in the sense that there will be assessment and sorting out. Judgement of this sort is a typical feature of the church's early preaching. If we look at Peter's summary of the gospel in Acts 10, we see that he runs briefly through the life and ministry of Jesus, but does not end with his death and resurrection. After the resurrection the last act includes the preaching of the gospel and what Matthew calls 'the coming of the Son of Man', (24:27ff); that is to say, the appointment of Jesus as judge (Acts 10:.42). We have the same pattern in Acts chapter 17 when Paul is preaching on the Areopagus (v.31).

To return to Matthew 24, the crisis in the first instance has to do with the destruction of Jerusalem in 70 C.E. It includes in due course the destruction of the Temple (v.2). Possibly the Temple here, as elsewhere in the Gospels, means the temple state and its government (compare Matthew 21:21), that is to say, the whole political system will be overthrown. There follows the proclamation of a number of false messiahs (v.5), wars and rumours of wars (v.6), and famines and earthquakes (v.7). The Jesus followers will be in a difficult position ('hated by all nations because of my name', v.9) because they will be neither on the side of the imperial government (the Romans) nor the nationalists (the Jewish insurgents). They are, as so often with non-combatants in time of invasion or civil war, in trouble with both sides. (Compare the fate of villagers who, during an insurgency, support neither the army nor the rebels.) Under this huge pressure there will naturally be those who 'fall away'; betrayal, confusion and mutual recrimination will be common (vs.10-12). The word of admonition is 'endurance'. If the time of crisis can be seen off, all will be well (v.13). In any case, none of this will prevent the widespread dissemination of the gospel (v.14). (Compare the events recorded in the Acts of the Apostles.)

Much of this may have already taken place in the experience of Matthew's readers, but he warns them that they may not, by any means, have seen the end. There is yet to be the climax to do with the Temple which is reminiscent of events in the time of Antiochus Epiphanes recorded in the Book of Daniel. At that time very special emergency measures will have to be taken because of the extent of the catastrophe (vs. 15-22). Once again there will be those who link these events with a Messianic visitation, but this is a deception (vs. 23-6). The 'coming of the Son of Man' will be something much more dramatic (v.27).

The sign of the (true) coming will be cataclysmic events in the heavenly realm which, in true apocalyptic fashion, will be answered by upheavals in the earthly realm. These will appear immediately after the events just mentioned, i.e. the desecration of the Temple and the destruction of Jerusalem and it will become clear that the old order has failed ('all the tribes of the earth will mourn' v.30). The Son of Man will henceforth be vindicated by the world-wide proclamation of the gospel (v.31).

To make sure that there is no mistake, Matthew warns his readers that these events have not yet taken place, but that they are just around the corner ('summer is near' v.32 and 'he is at the very gates' v.33) indeed this will take place within the lifetime of some of the hearers (v.34). Meanwhile the exact date is not available (v.36). What is available is a general warning that, taken as a whole, the end events can be described as 'the days of Noah' in which heedless people are rushing to destruction (vs. 37-9). Unlike the time of Noah, however, those who are alert can escape (vs. 40-1). Indeed the whole purpose of this discourse is that it should serve as a warning to Matthew's readers 'to keep awake' and 'be ready' (vs. 42-3). Parables follow to ram home the point (Matthew 24:45- 25:46).

Crisis at the end of the age

As we have said, these are notes for a time of crisis. For the first disciples of Jesus, and indeed for the whole nation of Israel, the events to do with the fall of Jerusalem were of extraordinary significance. For them it meant the end of the age. (For Jesus' followers the only event of equal significance was the unexpected spread of the gospel, as we have seen.) A modern equivalent might be what happened to the Jews in Nazi Europe. (See again Matthew 24: 9-13.) We do not know, writing in 2010, what *our* crisis might be, what might be the nature of 'the coming of the Son of Man' for us. Will it be something like environmental disaster? At the moment this seems more likely than not. Will it be unexpected war? War can still happen today, and bring terrible suffering and chaos. Ask the Iraqis. Will it be the spread of some unstoppable disease? We do not know. These matters are difficult to discern, impossible to forecast. The people of Noah's day were not aware that a *tsunami* was about to happen. Jesus' contemporaries may have felt that trouble was brewing, but they could hardly have foreseen the magnitude of the catastrophe. So it is that the warnings of coming trouble are as timely as ever, and along with the warnings go the appropriate survival instructions:

- Do not put your trust overmuch in human institutions (the Temple): look at what happened quite recently to massive and apparently secure banks and businesses;

similarly governments, however successful, do not last forever.

- Beware of false Messiahs. If you read Naomi Klein's *Shock Doctrine*[14] you will be reminded that there are plenty of ruthless operators who are only too happy to be busy within crisis situations and to take advantage of them to enhance their own power.

- Do not expect to be popular. You may even have warned people about climate change, for example, but do not count on their gratitude! In any case, Christians often find it difficult to take sides when there are crisis decisions to be made. Think of Bishop Bell in the Second World War who criticised the British government for bombing German civilians, and who ended up being unpopular with everyone.

- Do not be surprised if 'your enemies are those of your own household'. Persecution very often brings division and betrayal.

- Prepare for the long haul. Crises come suddenly, almost by definition, but they do not necessarily pass quickly.

- Even in the darkest times, the preaching of the good news is not an optional extra; indeed in dark times the light can shine more brightly.

- Though, as we have said, exact timings are not available, we can be *ready*. That, above everything else, is what the passage wants to say. Readiness is a mixture of watchfulness, spiritual fitness training, not being tied into 'the system' and getting on with kingdom tasks.

Security and risk

Matthew 24 has that edgy feeling that everything can be lost, but also everything can be saved. The Bible discourages the idea that security is normal. While, understandably, we usually strive to replace danger and helplessness by safety and control, we must also realise that the latter is ultimately illusory unless rooted in God. Also, as a response to danger, there are two sorts of behaviour, good and bad. Abraham does the risky thing. He sets out on a journey into the unknown and is commended for it. It demonstrates his faith in God. By contrast, King Ahaz (Isaiah 7-9) does what appears to be the prudent thing. He makes worldly-wise political arrangements and is condemned for it. They demonstrate his lack of faith. Situations of risk or danger can be a spiritual trap precisely because they can make people huddle together and emphasise their identity as against others. Fundamentalisms are examples of this sort of thinking and for the church it may lead to an even greater emphasis on maintenance rather than discipleship, a shrinking away from the real world and its dangers.

Discipleship, however, always entails leaving behind the familiar shelters.

A positive attitude to risk taking can be seen in a number of ways and these may help us in times of crisis. For example:

- 'Anything for a quiet life' is generally not thought to be a suitable motto for a Christian.

- Peter walking on the water is a good illustration, frequently used as a sermon illustration, for 'getting out of your comfort zone'.

- Jung said that the Beauty and the Beast archetype is perhaps the most significant one for human flourishing. Embracing the coming crisis is a sign of our confidence in God and a means of personal growth.

- There are people who are safe at home wishing that they were having adventures, and people having adventures wishing that they were safe at home. Apparently, the latter are the healthy ones.

A Scripture passage which may help us is Luke chapter 10, where we have the record of the mission of the seventy disciples commissioned by Jesus. They are sent out with the express orders not to take money or luggage with them, and not to greet anyone on the way (v.5). The implication is that there is extreme haste, and this gives us an important clue to the whole passage. The time is very short, there is extreme *urgency*, so much so that the messengers need to hurry past the people they meet on the road, like someone who bears a message that must be delivered swiftly to avert a disaster. (The battle has been lost, the enemy army is approaching; the gates must be closed and the walls manned immediately, if the city is to be saved.) Urgency demands risk. The disciples were to set out without back-up or supplies or equipment (which would have taken time to prepare) because the situation demanded immediate action.

Here again we have the familiar Biblical attitude to an approaching, probably disastrous, finale. The end is near; all the more reason for urgent activity. Luke 10 adds another dimension: if the end is near and the task urgent then more people must be recruited to do the work (verse 2); indeed, the task must be handed over to as many people as possible. Interestingly, the Greek text of Luke 10:1, when referring to the number of those sent out, reads both seventy and seventy-two. (The external evidence as to which is the correct reading is almost equally divided.) This is probably because there is a reference here to Numbers chapter 11 where seventy elders were chosen, but there was some dispute as to whether another two characters, Eldad and Medad, were to be added to their number. (See Numbers 11:16,17 and 26-30.) So this incident has to do with delegated leadership, which must be as generous as possible. When Eldad and Medad incorporated themselves in the leadership team, Joshua's first instinct was to exclaim, 'My lord Moses, stop them!' Moses' response was: 'Would that all the Lord's people were prophets, and the Lord would put his spirit upon them!' We can compare this with Luke 10:21 where Jesus rejoices that the task of bringing in the kingdom has been delegated to those who, on one view, were unsuited to the task. It is to 'infants', however, that Jesus has handed over the 'all things' that were originally gifted to him (10:22).

To make the obvious connection: we are in the same boat. If we are in an 'end time' we also have a message for our contemporaries. Because we do not have all the time in the world, its delivery requires greater urgency and more messengers than usual.

Community

Finally, to return to Slavoj Žižek, here is what he says about the church:

> Kant envisages a space of singular universality outside one's social identity. This appears in the New Testament as the Holy Spirit. It is described by Paul in Galatians 3:28. The Paulinian collective of believers is a proto-model of the Kantian 'world-civil-society'. It is the state which is the private sector.[15]

It is of crucial importance that in the coming catastrophe Christians stick together. It would be so good if the church as a whole could, as Žižek suggests, see its role as a universal witness. It would then recognise that the powers, including that power which is the state, are so many *private* interests, competing for their own survival, but not concerned in any real way, with the survival of the planet. I write this in the aftermath of the failed Copenhagen Conference, where it was only too obvious that governments were behaving as private entities, competing for their own interests, and that they *could* not therefore produce a global solution despite the fact that they had a global problem on their hands. On the first day of 2010, the *Guardian's* G2 supplement had the headlines: 'The politicians failed in Copenhagen: so now it's up to YOU.' It followed this up with 'the great Copenhagen cop-out has put the onus on individuals to step up the struggle against climate change' – an interesting switch from governments to individuals!

It is not easy to see how this would work. But if the church spoke with one voice, and was determined to act with one purpose, that would make a difference. It is the new Jerusalem that enters history to confront destructive Babylon. It is in the new Jerusalem that the tree of life grows, the leaves of which are for the healing of the nations (Revelation 22:2). We look around at the gathering storm and then at ourselves, a little band of confused and powerless people. It seems ridiculous to suggest that we can do much, and frightening to think that the future depends on us. But that is how it is. 'Do not be afraid, little flock', said Jesus to his disciples, 'it is your Father's good pleasure to give *you* the kingdom' (Luke 12:32). It probably seemed unlikely at the time that the little band of disciples that Jesus had collected together were the inheritors. But they were and so are we.

What does all this mean in practice? What is the way we should take? What can we do or say? Here are some suggestions.

Signs

As Lesslie Newbigin kept on insisting, the church is the *sign* of the kingdom.[16] If (local) churches are demonstrating kingdom life in such a way that people can actually look at them and see what God requires and the difference it makes, then they will repent and believe. For example, 'green' churches, which are actually taking the environmental agenda seriously, are the evidence that will convince people that there is another way of living beyond their wasteful and destructive lifestyles, a way that is more joyful, productive, healthy and just than anything that the Domination System offers. The first time that I heard Peter and Miranda Harris, the founders of *A Rocha*, the Christian environmentalist organisation, speak, somebody came to faith just by hearing them describe their work. 'Green' communities will preach for themselves.

Healings

When Jesus proclaimed the coming of the kingdom there followed widespread healing (Matthew 4:23-5 and parallels). Healing is what the kingdom brings. Many of the diseases which Jesus encountered and dealt with, were what might be called 'diseases of Empire'. They stemmed from the widespread violence of the age and the imperial economics that impoverished subject peoples. Many of our diseases today are similarly 'diseases of Empire'. Much of our poor physical health, along with the accompanying stress and depression, have to do with industrial growth and commercial exploitation. As the Empire, threatened by destruction, tightens its grip and yet also fails to protect us, we shall see more and more people being damaged by the system. This is what you might expect. In war zones people naturally get hurt. You might also add that hospitals become more than ever necessary.

Another way of putting this is that our churches must become 'cities of refuge'. Or again, the church is like Noah's ark when the flood comes, a particularly apt comparison because the ark saved not only the human race but the animals too. Ched Myers in his magisterial work *Who Will Roll Away the Stone?* identifies places that he describes as *heridas* (wounds) – military-industrial installations, strip-mines, huge dams, multiplying urban sprawls, gated communities, and, by contrast, *refugios* (communities of refuge) – monasteries, retreat centres, protest communities, small discipleship groups, agencies working against injustice.[17] (Myers 1994, 373-7). I suppose every local church should be a *refugio* while working against the *heridas*.

Exorcisms

An active assault on Babylonian ideology also seems necessary. At the heart of this lies the simple powerful statement that 'Babylon is fallen'. Of course, as the whole imperial system implodes, this will become increasingly evident. Even so, we need to bear witness now that the values by which Babylon lives are not those by which we can sustain life. The church's praise of God should be 'casting out' the praise of Mammon. Examples of simple liturgical statements that pull down Satanic strongholds can be found in Matthew chapter 4, where Jesus, drawing on the Deuteronomic tradition, speaks powerful sentences of opposition to an acquisitive and power-hungry worldview. 'One does not live by bread alone, but by every word that comes from the mouth of God'. 'Do not put the Lord your God to the test.' 'Worship the Lord your God, and serve only him.' (Matthew 4:4, 7, 10).

Memories

I have already said why I think memories are so important, but in a church or Christian community, our most important memory work happens in a eucharistic context. From the point of view of those facing disaster, the great eucharistic word is 'renewal'. We are told that it was 'on the night when he was betrayed' that Jesus inaugurated the commemoration (1 Corinthians 11:23). Human failure is therefore the first circumstance we are invited to think about, and this is important because when we struggle with the knowledge that things are getting progressively worse and hope is diminishing, our natural reaction is to blame other people. But despite the reality of suffering as a result of other people's behaviour – Jesus really was about to be betrayed, and knew it – it is not what Jesus wanted to talk about. Instead he promises that he will not take another Passover meal until it is fulfilled in the kingdom of God (Luke 22:16). He assures his disciples (and us) that whatever disasters might follow, the feast of the kingdom cannot finally be postponed. Whenever we celebrate the Lord's Supper, hope flares up again, even in the direst circumstances, and it does so because we reactivate our memories of that first event and the promise it contains.

Memory in this case is a *corporate* affair. The celebration of the Lord's Supper, like all good celebrations, is something we do with other people. Notice how Jesus says that the great joy of the occasion is that he is able to keep the Passover with his disciples (Luke 22:15). We are returned here to the idea of a reunion. Jesus wants to share the meal with these particular people precisely because it is they who have seen it through with him up to this point.

Effective, lasting, bonding relationships happen among those who are part of the same family and share a common place, with all its memories and associations, especially, perhaps, when they have been through bad times together. Thus the Israelites in exile are exhorted to remember their family connections (Isaiah 51:2) and also a particular place, in this case their capital city (Psalm 137). They weep when they are separated from their beloved homeland (verse 1), and are encouraged to 'remember Jerusalem' (verses 5, 6). So when disaster strikes we need to cherish our memories and we need to do this *together*. Any group which has misplaced its memories is about to cease to be a group. Nor can we survive as scattered individuals. Psalm 1 describes the rootless chaff which is blown away and contrasts it with the rooted tree which stands firm. Jeremiah 17 adds that such a tree has nothing to fear 'when heat comes' and 'in the year of drought'.

Conclusions

So how will it all end? We do not know and, in any case, that may not be the right question, though it does seem clear that we cannot go on as we have before. What must we do, however, is clearer.

First of all, there is the difficult matter of issuing warnings. The trends are all pointing in the same direction so we must stop pretending that they are not. This means refusing to be apathetic, or fatalistic, or triumphalistic and urgently calling our civilisation to an open-eyed realism, however unpopular that might be.

It is not just talk but action, of course. This is our God-given world. It is our home, the place where we can learn to be truly human. As Wendell Berry says, 'what we love we defend'. Every endeavour that nurtures our world and tries to prolong its existence is God's work. In the very teeth of catastrophe we can be building, planning, offering another way.

We must learn the end-time rules. There is plenty in the Bible about this. What does it mean to live a risky life, to exchange security for justice?

We need to come together, to look around for allies and start creating communities. Is it too dramatic to say that night is falling? Perhaps so. But it is certainly darker than it used to be. All the more reason to shine more brightly. 'You are the light of the world' said Jesus. Together we can keep the night away until a new day dawns.

References

1 S. Žižek, *First as Tragedy, Then as Farce* (London: Verso, 2009) p. 149. Zizek may have borrowed his illustration from the American poet, Robert Lowell.

2 ibid p. 151

3 ibid pp. 92-3

4 ibid p. 91

5 G. B. Caird, *Saint Luke* (Harmondsworth: Penguin, 1963) p. 121

6 C. S. Lewis, *Prayer: Letters to Malcolm* (Glasgow: Fount, 1977) pp. 120-4

7 This and the following quotation are taken from The Waterboys' album *A Rock in a Weary Land*. The track in question is 'The Wind in the Wires'. The lyric is by Mike Scott.

8 C. S. Lewis, *The Last Battle* (London: The Bodley Head, 1958)

9 W. Wink, *Naming the Powers* (Philadelphia: Fortress, 1984) p.5

10 D. Lessing, *The Making of the Representative for Planet 8* (London: Granada, 1980)

11 W. Benjamin, *Illuminations* (London: Pimlico, 1999) p. 249

12 Žižek p. 94

13 W. Wink, *Engaging the Powers* (Philadelphia: Fortress, 1992) Part one

14 N. Klein, *Shock Doctrine* (London: Penguin, 2008)

15 Žižek pp. 105-6

16 L. Newbigin, *Sign of the Kingdom* (Grand Rapids: Eerdmans, 1980)

17 C. Myers, *Who Will Roll Away the Stone?* (Maryknoll: Orbis, 1994) pp. 373-7

Lightning Source UK Ltd.
Milton Keynes UK
UKOW021530031111

181407UK00001B/1/P

9 780956 594303